FORTUNA REDUX

Faith Ellington

Praise for *Fortuna Redux*

Ellington's poetry articulates the day-to-day in the way a skeleton is articulated: eloquent joints, livid sinews, miraculous motion among the bones. Fortuna Redux offers an anatomy of what it is like to inhabit the emergencies, epiphanies, and agonies of daily breathing. By turns transcendent and merciless, these poems trace the remarkable wreckage of living in a world too precariously glittering to navigate without being carved up by its cruelty and wonder.

Chris Barrett, Phd

Concerned with language, place, the self, the body, Faith Ellington's Fortuna Redux builds an all-consuming world brick by brick, syllable by syllable. "Red words inhaled backwards/ on the roof of my mouth," she writes, and readers will be inhaled with them into these devouring poems.

Ariel Francisco

From the faux-private language of furtive search engine queries to the recalcitrant code of the othered, medicalized body, Faith Ellington's refiguration of lyric spirals galactically outward, fracturing and welding and fracturing again. "(something was done to me)," confesses the speaker in "Syntaxing": consider Fortuna Redux a smashing-open of parentheticals to reveal the unconscious like a shell-less egg. An intrepid debut, brash and melismatic—as full of serpents' hisses and cymbal crashes as the imperceptible music of algorithms singing each to each.

Andrew David King

Gnashing Teeth Publishing
242 East Main Street
Norman AR 71960
http://GnashingTeethPublishing.com

Printed in the United States of America

ISBN 978-1-966075-06-6

Non-Fiction: Poetry

Gnashing Teeth Publishing First Edition

Table Of Contents

PART I: METANOIA

https://duckduckgo.com/?q=bad+habits+or+addiction%3F&a+b=v112-1_y&ia=web

Resisting lingerie resisting chapstick call from a burner never
A landline too slow to disconnect splintered
Knuckles doctor winds up until
I can do it myself
Orange hospital pill bottle glow *please don't give me fentanyl*
Snow piles up Erie January wasteland in a shoebox
Baby, what do you think this is
Smudged face ruined mirror reverse
Edging towards hysteria assisted upon insistent on
Cool white lights bright pills under tongue
Heartbeat muddies under sternum chest
Under 54th street lamplit the sky unknits itself
Weatherman says *it cannot be possible*
Lake waves break frozen onto crackling sand

I & the body bleeds. The body twists itself into her knife.
The lungs fill with pitch, cold water swelling deep &
I dream of forcing the body into sleep. Her dreams tinged
Red to the root, bloody fingernails on the hand. Pick a face
For the body tonight & I will match it. The body divides itself
Into healing. She walks in front of the speeding car & I watch
Over the body. Hold the body steady against memory of twinned
Face, I slip tears down her cheeks. I & the body choreograph
Muscle memory of living. I & the body cannot wake
Her up. She & the body as surgical amphitheater. She carves
I & the body bleeds into she. Pick a self for the body
Tonight & I will match it. Blame redslick on our
Palms, the self somewhere between, razored sharp.

DEADBOLT

no one home to unslump body from bathroom floor / under sink basin
curl around pipes and reach slide / lock tumbler into place undisturbed taps
rush hot and cold into porcelain cream smooth / hands through hair until
flyaways lay straight stand / up let dread settle in fingertips pressed into
palms bracing against / vulnerability consider the faucet consider the
cracking of skull into curve / firm metal the force it would take to straighten
up and slam skull / again into faucet spatter brainbits and pop blood vessels
again /again cracked dribble until quiet outside the locked bathroom door

Bleeding bread: bacteria flush against palate spits rust all over
Finger probes ooze, wound drips onto blanched cloth altar
Take divinity in the mouth the molars the miracle cushioned
In a wafer delicate blood tucked under the tongue, soft.

METAPHYSICAL INTERIOR WITH BISCUITS

slab leaning untoward
rigid stripes parallel ceiling
floor wall panel nailed
together wooden curves
bouquet against foreground
two eyes three lines
a staring, a mouth
everything placed
all wrong

MINOTAUR

My neighbor's yard: fenced
Wooden slats, metal twining
Upwards from enclosure. Centered
In their half acre: a buffalo.
Odd pet for a Pennsylvania home
50 feet off the road so
Gentle or exhausted the huge
Creature lying prone blinking
Wetly towards the hot summer sky.

SYNTAXING

Painted German sunset
Oozes over my tongue
I consider passive voice
(something was done to me)

Standing cliffside
Watching barges lurch past
Let active voice dictate
Sinking feelings of guilt
(I did this)

Trees stand
Stupefied scars
It is (is it not)
My fault

Sunsetbargeswoods

The stain on my hands
Always my own or I am
A foreign body

(I oscillate)

ZOOK'S 8 POINT STAR

Hammer to pry nail out of side
Of shed, pry nail out of center
Of the hex: sign of the 8 point star
Which stands for sun, rain, fertility,
Hex sign watches over the shed
And the flat yard and the house
Windows watch sun and rain
And children playing in the green
Yard. 8 point star weatherstained
Until gray until cottontails
Under shed stop birthing litters,
Grass kneehigh devout girls
Pray for rain and when the yard
Is dry as a rattle, pry the hex off
The shed and pray for a guiding sign

DOWNSIZING

Blue wheelbarrow belly thick with ice
Layers of photographs frozen warped
Stacked all but invisible under translucent
Ice except for one. Recto: gangrenous corpse
Middle-aged man bloated purpled
At least 72 hours gone, burned by a son
With a penchant for arson and patricide
I think. My father can't remember anymore
All the polaroids in evidence old case photos
Blown up and printed on poster board for
Courtroom sessions. He either clinched a prosecution
Or didn't. So many years, so many *Commonwealth of Pennsylvania vs.*
Now we are left to dispose of the evidence:
Burn, shred, freeze. Some copies are still on file
Some copies ashed in our fireplace some copies
Frozen in our wheelbarrow waiting for thaw waiting
To be congealed then dried out and scraped pulpy like
Confetti into a trash bag placed on the curb come one Monday
In spring.

6TH AND PENN

Bureaucracy in the faces of unfortunate:

Can you advise on what to do?
A very small circle has punctuated our glass
And glass is on the floor and on the sidewalk and
I have to file a claim...

Bullet hole in my favorite cafe window shattered
Or perhaps conchoidal fractured around a single point
Breakage from pointillism, of course
There's a center to all fallings apart
Or more to the point: there's a
Point in how things break
Anyway, the Reading Eagle never reported
A break-in or a shooting at the cafe,
And how did the cafe report the bullet
To the insurance claim?
Sometimes things can't be accounted for.

PAX RIVER [& OTHER PLACES]

Before we cursed each other
I swam in Pax River
& other places
Drifting down
The water column
Glimmering sand kickback
Sunburn taut on shoulders
Lungs swelling on dock
Worn cotton towels stretched over sand
Flipping over swells
Searching for riversmooth glass
Water pooled in clavicle wells
Laughing, photographs, eyes shut

XCROSSINGX

Finally: winter.
Boots lug soles
Bandaid heels
Walk in night.
Yellow lamps
No stars.
A mile down
The long road
Gas station coffee.
Hazelnut with cream
Cinnamon with sugar.
No change.
Walk through night.
Heat blooms in chest.
Finally: quiet.
Houses flicker dark
Pass over railroad
Tracks: exhale.

PORTRAIT OF MY OLDER SISTER AS OZYMANDIAS

I transcribe our phone calls (

Compulsion to

record) & I think about the heaviness

Of us, my sister and I,

turned to stone by our worrying.

I hold my sister's problems /

rip the pages up.

I place them in strangers' hands

Look at her the fragments demand.

Remember her so I don't have to do it all myself.

That quirk of paper her legacy,

That quirk of paper mine.

ACTIVE/PASSIVE [VOICE]

sleep in my childhood bed: wonder at what happened to me.
peel off duvet & fitted sheet & look at the mattress:
look at the stains. acknowledge or forget.
which time? watch the green glowing clock in the corner:
time drags its feet or evaporates. the walls are just the same. lay in my bed
shivering. it's summer. i grew up very much alone: understand i carved
isolation. never does well to dwell in self-pity: won't anybody notice? no—
i was too clever or not hurting enough. which was it?
& now i can't stand to be touched. i sit in my bed:
dwindle hours away as if they are painful things and not gifts.

CENTRALIA, PA

a god's honest ghost town on fire beneath my soles on
grimy layer of graffiti over cracked asphalt road over
coal seam enflamed and predestined to burn for
o, the next several hundred years (or so)

pass mailbox mouths agape
as houses relent into earth all the while
rocking chairs rot & porch lights are hanged from solitary chains

dwindled down town dissolved by overundergrowth
& still I see a man mowing the lawn though no
one is supposed to live here. Population: 5
(I read online)

coal country is coalfire country is sinkhole country too
area supposedly secured after sinkhole exhaled hot air
into Centralia's streets, citizens made aware their land
was on fire right beneath them:

this is coal country and we know the risks even more
than we know the process of eminent domain and condemnation
limestone sacrificed to oxygenation

that forced flight— I walk around in it
roads paved through an empty zip code
eyes alert to toxic smoke & we know the rumors-turned-fact
some places are uninhabitable after human error
coalfire raging already for sixty years apocryphal
town suspended over uncauterized coal vein

(place palm on earth &
expect the earth to be warm but it is not
expect the earth to scorch you but it will not
fire embedded far below, danger still)

PORT ELIZABETH, NJ

The tide swings around
The island to the Bay's outer tip

Tangling breezes mix
Marsh (sucking mud,
Salty grass, brackish decay)
Ocean (clean salt,
Taut sunshine, dune grass)

Greenheads bite tender skin
On ankles
Behind ears
Trailing swollen welts

Lime taffy green
Amoxicillin pink
Knock-kneed houses
On algaed stilts

The tide dredges
In this morning
Horseshoe crab tails
Shattered turtle shells
A seagull with no eyes

Under sand-worn
Summer soles
Plucked seaglass

DRESSING ROOM

At the very back of the dress, a wound
A peeling away of green fabric until
Dulled skin rippled by scars by curvature
Of spine. Deep breathing unseals scabs, leaks
Red onto the floor. My mother, crying:
You could have been so beautiful. My hands:
Bonethin and scrabbling for sharpness.

PEASANT FAMILY IN AN INTERIOR

Thimble of red wine between forefinger and thumb
Bent brows cleave sallow face holy as a mother,
Watching and showing no teeth. Pewter pitcher dull
Against olive drab and sooty firelight. Children cluster
Around tin flute, sickly cat, empty ladle. Legs curved by
Rickets, children sit on floor scrubbed clean for portrait
Sitting. Boychildren wear threadbare gray brown,
Girlchildren have hair covered by white. Mother watches
The painter. In the corner: raw hand clutches bread, knife.

WARM WINTER

Each year closes like a mercy
I bury it: deep
Water slips no sound

Floodlights overflow kitchen
Sink against my back bite
Into my ripe mouth

Muscle sinew skin knit
I was created I will rest
I disfigure myself

Yes, live a day:
Dirt under fingernail
Don't consume as before

Fate is a gift;
Walk on knees: beg:
Take it all from me

ANGEL #

The rapture called and
I missed — the call dropped
My purse on the bed threw
Away my lipstick.

In hell or high water I
Make coffee and drink from
Same gray mug stare
Out the chickenwire windows.

Stitches like a black caterpillar
Wriggle across forehead I
Prick my thumb as often as
Gridded cloth I sew color into.

Mirror turned to face the wall
After death but now all the time
Plush drapes rigid over underwire
I knot all my bedsheets into rope.

https://duckduckgo.com/?q=reducing+scarring+appearance&atb=v112-1_y&ia=images

Morphine eyes kissed by anaesthesiologist
Clock ticks in at 11:30 to wake up crying
Even though postsurgically I am numb
Doctors inspect bleeding and inspect hysterical aspects of my nature
Perhaps I *wanted* my stitches to catch and tear and rip a hole in me, no?
Thick bumpy tissue has not risen out of thinly clotted incisions
I cannot wash my hair for one week, that is
I cannot wash my hair for seven days although
Insurance rings and rings says
I *owe* them what I did not pay
Clatter rattle of bottles turned inside mirrored cabinet
Hungry eyes for opioids and quick cash I refuse
I know I am lucky although
I drive until blood drips through my shirt
Body not done healing for a whole summer
Still numbness tugs on chest struggling to feel and/or hurt

NEUROTROPICAL

Baker Act me into an induced vacation
Whitened smell of bleach and clothes too soft
Insurance asks me to pay them in blood
Money and my psychopharmacologist is scrawling
Out more bills. Pills. Whoops. Court-ordered
Therapist tilts an understanding head to the side
We have some things we need to discuss, but:
Bills. Insurance lapsed once I was found to be a leech.
Trying to balance my act together while balancing
Financials. Not here by choice; can't afford to get it together.

THE GROSS CLINIC

Thomas Eakins, cut me open—
What would make it onto the canvas?

Dissection unfurls
body & genetics spiraling towards fate:
Decisions epigenetic predestination, choice

Surgical instruments excavate flesh
Fail to bisect
Genetic inheritance
& my own decisions
Start over &
Still my body clings to me

Eakins does his best to dissever my body
But the problem is too deeply imbedded

Eakins will turn to the gallery and declare
I have wasted his time

My body a wound so grotesque
It cannot possibly be self-inflicted

KARLOVA TÕUSEB

I walk Karlova in the rain
Watch slick streets dissipate heat,
Water rising as ghost into June air

Past the Soviet apartment buildings, gray
Identical, all watching eyes
Smoke drifting out of windows
Radio down low leaking onto street

Past the old grocery store
Yellowed with graffiti as broken glass
Gives permission to peer in through chicken wire
Wound tight against intrusions

IN THE SAME VEIN

Laying
      in a field

Drawn and quartered

Cornea sky

Looks down from
      St. Peter's gate

Joints now loosened
      limb from limb
            broken matchsticks

Red words inlaid
      backwards
            on the roof of my mouth

I rot and wait

For ninebark to close the wounds

When dawn descends
      I can't decide which is more cruel:

Barbed wire or an electric fence

HITCHHIKER [GHOST]

Sit right beside me and we are hitchhiker, ghost.
State lines speed limits blur as we tip
Into Indiana, Illinois. Midwest winter glittering
Harsh under gray sun. Under eyes violet grip
The steering wheel with windchapped knuckles
& stare at the number on the house, reconciled with
+1 (309)-XXX-XXXX. Car heater dries out our mouth
We turn the radio low, we have to make a decision.
Lights on in the house can either of us feel
Justified through cracked frost on the windshield.
I used to sleep in Walmart parking lots
So I wouldn't have to deal with this shit.
Snow sticks. Time evaporates. Winter pools at our feet.
Baseball bat / slashed tires / crowbar / bloody knuckles / revenge fantasy
House door opens & outside of us *he* smokes under the porchlight
We sit side by side & stare at the end of the story
We know: turn the car around & go home.

HELP//ENCLOSURE//HELP

Poor little Lazarus who had to die
Twice. Who had to walk through that cold
Room and into the dark all over and over
Again. Twisted proportions of a second life
Birthless, singular. What could he have asked
Of God instead? Synoptically unrooted could never
Die— He re-lived and never breathed, Lazarus.
What breaks your heart.

BEDDING SCHEMES

What have I what have I done in the garden
Sculpted into rooms without scent without
Ceiling the hardy plants slashed into topiary
I wanted a kitchen garden and ended up with
Twelve laborers coaxing iron ribs of greenhouse
Sweated soil harvests yew rough palms on stone walls
My particular narrow-leaved lavender imported delicate
Stems knotted into thematic creatures watching
Fuchsia garden crystallized ponds, O precise vistas
Built up by another, beardtongues sprawling into beds
Under my feet there must be earth I have to ask
Stripped from wire trellis how could I possibly live

TARTU, ESTONIA

Houses weep at me
Singe-smoke from wood burning stoves leaks
A pinpoint at the base of my throat, trapped
Feeling something soft & unwanted

Dark days with slim sun no stars
Every day a day to start over
To look up at the sky and see blank
Forever

Matchstick houses collapse & form a flat horizon
Row on row on row
Loosened ice floats in the mouth
Too early, yet, for thaw

SKIN BUBBLE

needle slides under dermis releases tuberculosis antigen no more than ⅝ of
an inch into the skinfatmuscle tissue

redness at injection site is normal; bruising at injection site is normal; small
bump from needle entry point is normal;

swelling of the skin into a raised bubble signals a body already compromised,
skin bubble rigid with promise of contagion

watch for 48 hours; watch for 72 hours; watch hands running over injection
site soft skin hands praying to feel smooth flatness; please; please;

YOU ARE THE SALT OF THE EARTH.

Watcher. Eyes like a lamp in the dark.
Hand of the almighty wills scorched earth.
Who can stand and face wrath?
Burning city reeks of judgment. Sin prodded out like
Cattle. To be spared is to wander into night:
Eyes rolling toward darkness. Cast out into
Palm of the deliverer. Smell of acrid flesh
Behind. Wail of ashen throats behind.
The spared, unpreserved bend on blistered knees.
Face heavy under veil of smoke, will anyone
Watch over the burning. Gaze turns back.

Gather up the leftover fragments so that nothing will be lost

After miracle, leftover

Loaves soften to mold

Fish eyes crust in delicate sockets

Scales flake off like so much wasted glitter

Baskets heavy with scrap

Odor mingles with desperation

BITTER ANGEL, JUBILANT KNIFE

Feel like ugly meat as I drop to my knees—
Begging desperation erupts as blush over
The bones in my face carved into grief—
Hands forced into prayer I seek out
Protection. Comfort. Skinned knees
Gather clumps of sand in their opening,
Red stains on the grains when I rise off the dunes.
Beyond the grasses ocean watches serrated.
Pink pearlescent wound of my mouth closed.
Who will pray for me, mean it:
My raw salt heart.

PART II: RIGA SEQUENCE

[RIGA] ETYMOLOGIES

Riga. etymology uncertain: perhaps corrupted liv word for *loop*, reflecting the shape of its harbor. perhaps from the latvian word for threshing barn. perhaps from latin *rigata*, meaning irrigated. as in: pagan latvians were forcibly converted by mapmaking christians supposedly *irrigating* dry pagan souls with the waters of christ's baptismal font.

to keep myself from thinking about Riga, here's what i do: i build a wall. unlike its baltic counterparts, Riga is not a walled city. i picture mixing the cement, hands steady, stacking bricks. mortar, smoothed. habitual actions, i focus on those, on how to build a wall that cannot breached. the bricks are wide and tall, but not heavy. i labor at building a wall until i slip into this frame of mind automatically.

q: *did you tell anyone?*
a: [   ]

when building a wall doesn't prevent me from Riga, i imagine burying an iron safe under the soft earth. metal shovel light in my arms, i tamp down the soil. i try to pretend the safe is under a wide wheat field where it will not be reaped. see: when the wall doesn't work, i get desperate.

q: *and what was the nature of your relationship to [* ███████ *]? how would you describe him?*

but of course nobody asks me that, and i cannot answer. but if someone were to one day ask me and if one day i could answer, i could start with the word *brutal*. first recorded use in the fifteenth century. from latin *brute*, translating literally into heavy + the middle french *brut*, meaning rough. brutal, originally used in reference to beasts, sometimes with a religious undercurrent [see: john milton]. derivatives include: brutality. as in: the *brutalities* of a prison. as in: beast buried inside a labyrinth of walls. as in: life without an escape.

DESENSITIZATION/REPROCESSING/PINE/
DESENSITIZATION/REPROCESSING/PINE/

Years later sap scent sharp catches the breeze
Triggers: My body in Helsinki
Airport dwindling away a layover staring
At wide white windows the snow banks
Covering the base of the pines white sky
Presses down the only color comes from
Pitch-black pines bending to winter
Nothing else moves

Bus delivers my body to its fate across
A small country looking at the window looking out
The window at white fields copses of houses
Staccato kruschyevska dwarfing the bus the body
Sitting straight as a pine

Gray floors scrubbed until blank blue
Bucket sits reeks of cleaner smells like pine fresh air
Apartment window open onto gray buildings contemplate
In movies blood dries red though it is obvious to us
That blood dries brown

Frame silhouette tall all shadows lean
Against doorframe despite all cruelty
Hesitancy in the angle breath stilled before
Entry in the bedroom furniture constructed cheaply
Out of cheap wood someone said it was a kind of pine
Splinters easily is given to rot

No— My body sitting on a dock wind ruffles grass lightly
Under bluer sky feel wood warm under body
Air goes in through the nose out through the mouth
A dissociative space I float safely towards, cool green water
But no—

The mouth of the woods across the lake is dark a gap in the pines
Gaping blackness tip face forward stare very hard at the edge of the woods
And wait

SIMULACRUM

I'm not a dog
Right before you slam my head into the wall. You leave me and I go home.

The summer blisters onward. My mother my sister and I stand on cool
kitchen tiles barefoot
The screens straining in cicadas and hot air. I stand still. My sister making
lemonade. My mother says I'm so glad I raised children who would never
stand for abuse. What she doesn't know won't kill her.

My older sister calls me in the Rite Aid parking lot I sit down right between
the cracked white lines
Orange streetlights keep me from getting run over. She tells me what I
already guessed.
It's in the way we can't make eye contact.

August and my older sister and I sleep on an air mattress. I say if you marry
him I'm going to cut off my pinky finger like that crazy lady we saw on TV
and I'm not kidding. Sometimes my sister looks at me and I wonder what she
knows about me or has guessed.

The basic question: what's going to happen to us?
All year I become what I am not and I chirp like a songbird *don't touch me*
don't touch me don't touch me

THE TIMES WE HAD are etched into my right shin, so much so that months later my mother asked if I had been burned. How to explain it? Glossy mark, stretched tight over tibia, necessitates white lies. Hours spun around my leg, sterile cotton bandages, waiting for that gully to stitch itself together. I know how to care for a wound. Sun setting lightly on astringent bandages, took weeks until the cut would stop cracking open, leaking me all over the floor. I watched the skin darken as it forced itself to scab, heavy effort struggling against mechanical pressure. Eventually new scar tissue formed discolored, clotted purple. Time expired: You left, then I did. Empty apartment, skin on my shin turned sickly white. I learned quickly to favor my left leg and to convince myself that closure exists beyond the dermis.

STRAWBERRY SWINGIN'

& forever & forever you run on a loop in my head. A Norfolk Southern breeze blows through and with it, lanternflies. Where are we? Sign says WELCOME 2 WHISKEY DITCH. You are static on the radio, concurrent with the aux cord playing something sweet. Sweet Life. We are summer solstice angels, I am writing you a love poem, you make my skin crawl. & count how many lanternflies have dropped into our hair, a crown. & waterboard me in the river & I won't stop shaking, my fingernails hurt, can't sleep. Sharpen my teeth. Let me correct myself: You make my coffee just right: honey, cinnamon. Let me correct you: get off of me. & too hot to sleep in the attic so you crawl under my skin. Our bones intertwined. & you are my whole summer, rotted pitted fruit & I still love you. How do you do it? Train whistle blows, you glow for me. Catch fireflies, let them go. We run parallel. We are the same train line. Hold me while I grow wings, while I surgically remove your teeth. & this is what it was. Who we were. Should've known. Shouldn't have made you blackberry lemonade. Lanternfly legs as toothpicks, stuck between teeth. A plague. Should've said don't touch me. We pick strawberries, buttercup yellow bruises spilled under tanned skin. & forever this summer runs under me, fused glass dream. Who cares if I can't wake up.

WHERE CAN I CARRY MY SHAME?

fingers flaked with flour, sweat, fluids
desperate to unravel threads carefully woven spun
into softness, a cocoon that failed, a shroud cruelly
visible. cloth torn apart, nails embedded in skin
below. long hallways, a girlhood silhouette, violent
unrobing as strips of sleeves float to the floor, wailing.

MEANDER SCAR

the emajōgi shifts under bridge he told me
he jumped off of and i prayed he did i
knew also that the bridge was too low
to jump and mean it i am an old player in
an old game he was gonna kill me or i was
gonna let him kill himself i got very good
at sitting still i got very good at our normal
emergency operator doesn't speak english i
can't afford another international call we
despise each other certainly we cannot
leave our gray room and walk over the city
and cross water without a pirouette into
current below this is so fucked up i know

NO LONGER BARS ON THE WINDOW:

Crows pick at the trash through thin ice

And I smell smoke. Shut the window and
        drop the blinds.
                Knife on the windowsill

Reminds me to still my breath and sit down—
        No. Stand up. On the edge of the bed with
                washed sheets and no key taped under bed frame.

Calculate under low ceilings: coffee, bread, the dead roach
        at the end of our bed. Pockmarked walls, playing house

Unwitnessed.
        I think about how to become plausible.

Not even dirt on the gray floor. Might as well be nowhere.

Blank portrait, wintered city with nobody in it.

What if the window drifts open, windowsill
        bleached and wide. Forget about the knife. Perch and swing
                tense legs into bitter April air. Someone's cigarette glitters

In the dark.
        All I have to do is wait for the door to open

        All I have to do is wait for your hand on my back,

ANGEL'S GLOW

& the sun goes down
Glowls lightly on clean cotton bandage;
Soft to medical gauze
How'd you get that wound?
Sliced up stitched together a badly-mended
Garment fluttering on the windowsill
Unspooled thread slack and frayed
When can stitches come out?
At night & spill my glowing guts all over the page—
What you've done in the dark
I've brought to the light

FOR ████

live my life backwards so it doesn't hurt & I already know the ending

I sleep facing the east let the sun break open onto my face spill
over my shoulder seep into the end of my dreams

dream into a mirror dream into verse how to write it all into a line
how to write ?

I already know the end of this poem. I already know the end of this line.

YOU'RE THE ONLY TWO PEOPLE I'D GET MATCHING TATTOOS WITH

Last night we walked to the river and we drowned. Right after
The three of us walked to the store starvingscared
I bought a can of lime coke
You bought a pouch of sour spaghetti
While you bought nothing, anxious
Threading through shelves, window avoidance, coins
Dull in our riversoaked pockets
We clung to each other
Each of us in turn faces crumpled—
The other two gathered close, held tightly
Couldn't bring ourselves to leave the aisles eyes watching
The outside, dread behind.
We hurt to each other in interior spaces
Triad of castaways fleeing clutching each other to our chests
Even as we slipped out of safety: water

Gallicolumba luzonica

(I can't sleep when you're in the house
When we lay in the dark and stare
I have to get out, walk, blisters rise & burst)
So cold outside that my exhalations can only freeze
Chest hurting in two-time step: cold air seepage and some sort of bruising
Walk around with blood dripdripping through a thin t-shirt
Can you hear me okay?
Press into the gore of the wound, blood embedded under fingernails
scraping sternum
I think there's something wrong, I think—
Kneel on sidewalk so cold my knees ache
I confess:
No, I'm okay, I think my chest is just bleeding...
You don't need to send anybody, I can walk just fine,
Frost whips my face into shape, o the shame!
Steady pulse to slow trickling blood
Try to stand even as heartbeat crawls
Do you get these kinds of calls a lot?
Speck of blood spatters onto frozen slab of sidewalk
Do you know the name of what's happening to me?

RIGA, LATVIA

I missed the bus
For violence

Mosaic room
Bars on window
Knife on windowsill

A cherry-sized bruise
On my wrist waits to tell me the time

No clock
No phone to call
Anyone (or you)

Gray bus station
Riga → Tartu

You stare out the window
I stare at the floor

GENUFLECT

Incense rattle of smoke through another Russian Orthodox church glimmering gilded & I kneel, as I am supposed to, cross myself the right way (right to left). Slush of Russian words: *stand*. But I bring to kneel. Saints. Apostles. Eyes watch, painted and benign in immobility. I cannot read Cryllic script, I can nearly tell the bearded weeping men apart as they stare at me. Horror. Accusation. Ephesians: *It is shameful to mention what the disobedient do in secret*. & I drift to the way I was looked at by you / (in Riga) you wept. Wrath. & in Riga I sat on the edge of our bed. Still. Genesis: I know Abraham put down the knife. The knife stayed on the windowsill. Even I cannot confess what happened. Answer this: how did Isaac look at Abraham when it was over. How did I look at you. Horror. Accusation. Yes— even after, I sat with you in our bed. *Nozh.* Kneeling / Turn my gaze back to arched ceilings, my mind to the priest amidst painted alters. What good is mercy if the hand still reached for the knife? I kneel or I sit. I cannot stand myself.

GOOD WOMAN

Because I let your blood overflow the sink because I towel dry your hair after you drown yourself in the bath. The doctor at the ER slips numbing needle under my skin tells me good girl when he's done stitching. My father calls me a cup of black coffee. Because I forget to remind myself that you said okay (I'm sorry) after I said *stop*. I know you didn't mean anything by it; I'm your good woman. Because I kept you alive, because you told me I noticed. Because I bought you a bottle of gin and told you to kill yourself, because I straitjacketed you, because we drink iced Americanos. We text each other back, I buy you lunch in the park, we deserve good weather. The armbruise was so ugly, so ugly that I asked about it. Where's the thread? I can see bone. I'm your good woman.

ASTRINGENT

Pull the bandaid off my shoulder & ease
Into a cold sleep, window open

& if I don't wake up then
I am a walking dream of getting shot in the stomach
Radial fractured viscera seeping

Won't you hold my hand? Or you don't like me
Like this, congealed blood spattered on scapula

Visions of gunshot wounds ringing in my head—
I understand

Laid bare & shivering
Hands reaching for wounds that do not have permission to exist

I would never ask you to stay

LOVE LETTER FROM LIÈGE

Because I think about Rimbaud like this:
Not an *enfant terrible* but a young man whose lover
Shot him in the wrist in a rage in a hotel room

When I turn Liège over in my mind I reflexively
Ask who cleaned Rimbaud's blood off the walls? The sheets?
What color was the gauze wrapped around his wound?

The bullet wasn't removed from Rimbaud's wrist for 9 days
& he eventually withdrew his police complaint against Verlaine

Rimbaud completed his work after the wound-
ing. The title of which translates into
A Season in Hell

I want to know: what was the physical act of writing like
Given the serious nature of Rimbaud's wound?

After, he wrote in *"Angoisse:" rouler aux blessures, par l'air lassant et la mer* in
Agony: let me roll in my wounds, through the heavy air and the sea

I hate that I reduce Rimbaud to this:
Injured, bleeding at the hands of an alcoholic man he trusted

& I fear this scene duplicates, triplicates, slips
Into the experiences of mine until I forget
These wounds are serious—

Just because he shoots you when you try to leave
Doesn't mean he loves you

TEDDY BEAR KNIFE

Through the body: I understand the fragments afterwards. No— that's not right. I understood them even as they were happening, even as you stood over me and I sat on the bed.

Well— I know you. You rest easy, you sleep sprawled out behind unlocked doors. My quiet painkiller sleep.

I need to get a grip or maybe just hold on tighter to what I scraped together: call it memory.

PERIAQUEDUCTAL GRAY

Forever & a fever: I slept through the whole spring/I slept buried in the parking lot under the gravel. Someone closed my eyes while I slept. Was it your leaving that did it? Come July, I thawed back into my body, permissioned at last. We all came to our ends/no one else could have done what I did: *For I do not understand what I am doing. For I do not do what I want – instead, I do what I hate.*

[7 MONTHS AFTER] RIGA, LATVIA

Riga wires my jaw shut I sit on the curb
My older sister will not take off her jacket
It is February but it is 70 degrees. I think if I
Could just reach out and touch us:
Scrape my fingernails against asphalt I wonder
At how to speak it all the knife hovers over
Our heads we are both tired of flinching. I hold
No one accountable but myself. I take off my hoodie.
Molars worked smooth we sit in silence
On the curb I scrape a gully in my right thumb.
In due time their foot will slip. Muteness swallows us whole.

PARANOIA

Called always eyes watching me called
Opening red door to find you
Inexplicably behind called
I saw you at an airport I saw you
At a bar I saw you on a street called
At least I thought I could recognize you
Called you're following her but called
Me you hold me against you
Against myself you texted me at 3:13 why called
You take your smoke breaks under my window you
Watch me watch smoke curl called
You know where I am you know who I am you
Know me

THIRD PARTY, BLIND

Remove blindfold and tip scales forward in horror:
Not enough to wander in the dark as metal clangs—
Weight of balancing acts uncloaks the neutral
To sit in judgment: to sit in sin: to sit beside
Oneself. Watch the hanging. Watch the hanging.
Drop the scales and reach for justice: bare brush of
A hand against robe renders a cure. A testament
If only the hand could reach if only the hand could
Loosen its grip on the noose if only the hand
Could slip its grip on the hanging.

THE ▮▮▮ GAME WAS ON

& so I left the bar. Couldn't take it. Walking home dead sober fantasizing
About getting my stomach pumped. Acid burning, the wrongness
Of being turned inside out. I walk home because the ▮▮▮ Game
Was on, four nail marks on each palm, layers of accumulation. Scar
Tissue to the dermis, drifting dunes of pressed pink lines, fine.
Not shy to violence. I walk home
And the look on my face is one I only recognize when a man
Waiting in his car for someone (a girlfriend?)
Catches sight of me and looks at me as one looks at a new griever.
He does not roll down his window. Numbed legs deliver me home.

JEZEBEL ASKS: WHERE IS THE PRINCE?

Indeed, where is he, as her body is thrown from window
By three men onto earth below snapped and whipped
Blood on the walls. Horses crush bones drag crust of organs
Through the city, rusted flaking trail. Jezebel: dog, bitch, whore. Hot
Breath leaks out of canine muzzles caressing warm corpse. Stripping
Off flesh slow to fill feral appetites. Jezebel cursing:
By this time tomorrow I will make your life
like the lives of those you killed. Jezebel cursed:
In the stomachs of dogs, a widow, unburied.
Under the window remains: a skull, two bloody feet,
Two lacerated palms. *Stigmata*: A mark of disgrace.

I think about it so much it's un/real until you're smoothed over with worry. I can't hold him in my head. Nowhere to go. As in, we went to go look for his body. Months. The view out the window: street, people. Apartment building, construction workers. Outside/inside sitting duck. As in, he led us to believe we needed to look for his body. What did I want to find/what did it mean to want a corpse. I wanted to find his body so that they wouldn't have to and also to make sure that he was dead. Hold the body to my chest. Snap the skull into the earth. Drown him again. Now I'm not so iron. Did I run to him no. Did I pull him to my chest no. Was I happy. How was I supposed to feel it. He went upstairs I felt the adrenaline leak out of the body/sat down. What did I do. Months/Months. I went to look for you/r body. Months. You/him. I. Months. *What happened in Riga?* We were there for three days iron on windows and it felt like months. Months later: body. In between drifts down: snow. Accumulation/months. Months.

FORTUNA REDUX

once I started remembering I couldn't stop. the exit wound in my head drops me onto a stretch of sand, ocean foaming around my ankles. I want to stop bleeding from an exit wound, I want to pray to anybody: can I find my way to a home. time to start again. if this is home, for now, can I think about what I know: salt is good for a wound. I have to stay for a while. how to measure time: hours/waves/hours/waves/ hours/waves [...]

References

"The Gross Clinic Scalpel" and "The Gross Clinic" draw their titles from
Thomas Eakins's *Portrait of Dr. Samuel D. Gross (The Gross Clinic)*

"Book of Miracles Folio 19" draws its title from the 16th century German
illuminated manuscript *Augsburg Book of Miracles*

"Metaphysical Interior with Biscuits" draws its title from Girogio de
Chirico's painting of the same name

"Zook's 8 Point Star" draws its title from Pennsylvania Dutch hex signs

"Peasant Family in an Interior" draws its title from the Le Nain painting of
the same name

"Karlova Tõuseb" is an Estonian phrase translating to "Karlova Rises."
Karlova is a neighborhood in the Estonian city Tartu.

"Gather up the fragments so nothing will be lost" references John 6:12

"Where Can I Carry my Shame" references 2 Samuel 13:13

"Gallicolumba luzonica" is the binomial name of the bleeding-heart dove

"Love Letter from Liège" takes its translation from Wallace Fowlie's
Rimbaud: Complete Works, Selected Letters Bilingual Edition

"Periaqueductal Gray" draws its title from a part of the brain involved in
pain control, emotional responses, and responses to threatening
stimuli. Within the poem, the lines "For I do not understand what I
am doing. For I do not do what I want – instead, I do what I hate." is
a reference to Romans 7:15

"[7 Months After] Riga, Latvia" references Deuteronomy 32:35 in its final
line

Acknowledgements

The following poems have appeared elsewhere:

"https://duckduckgo.com/?q=bad+habits+or+addiction%3F&a+b=v112-1_y&ia=web" *Fools Mag* (vol. 8), spring 2020.

"Syntaxing"; "6th and Penn"; "Toosday"; "Portrait of My Older Sister as Ozymandias" poetry series in *Sierra Nevada Review*, spring 2021.

"*The Gross Clinic* Scalpel" *Passengers Journal,* March 2022.

"Periaqueductal Gray" *Prometheus Dreaming*, spring 2022.

"Simulacrum" *Blood Tree Literature*, June 2023.

"[7 Months After] Riga, Latvia" *Mockingheart Review*, December 2023.

"HELP/ENCLOSURE/HELP" *Mockingheart Review*, December 2023.

"Downsizing" *Hole in the Head Review*, January 2024.

"Hitchhiker, Ghost" *Hole in the Head Review,* January 2024.

"Centralia, PA" *Keystone: Contemporary Poets on Pennsylvania* (Penn State University Press), January 2025.

About the Author

Faith Ellington received her PhD in English from Louisiana State University. Originally from Reading, Pennsylvania, she began her writing career at the University of Iowa. She currently researches and writes poems on the East Coast. You can find her work at faithellington.com.

www.ingramcontent.com/pod-product-compliance
Lightning Source LLC
Chambersburg PA
CBHW051330120626
46547CB00016B/2478